The Gift of Being Different

Written by **Monica Berg** Inspired & co-created by **Abigail Berg**

Illustrated by **Sonia Possentini**

SH

SPIRITUALLY HUNGRY
PUBLISHING

Hi! I'm Abigail. I'm 8 years old, and I just found out that I have a superpower.

What's it like to have a superpower?

Well, at the beginning it felt really lonely. I knew I was different because I had trouble reading in school.

During language arts, me and all the other students in my class work together in small groups.

Each group is a different color. I'm in the blue group, which made me really happy at first because blue is my favorite color.

Then I noticed that the yellow and green groups read more exciting books.

Me and the other blue group kids read books that are really pretty boring.

This made me sad because I love stories, especially ones with imaginary creatures in them, like dragons or griffins.

The yellow group kids do fun activities, and they get to talk a lot. I'm really good at talking, but me and the other blue group kids spend most of the time reading words.

I practice and practice, but reading is still really hard for me. We have to read sentences out loud, and when I read too slow, I can feel the other kids looking at me.

It makes my stomach feel swirly. My teacher told me to focus. But I was focusing. I concentrated so much on the letters and words that my head would start to hurt.

I know the letters. And I know the sounds. But it takes me a while to put them together. And sometimes, my brain flip-flops the letters, so it sounds wrong when I try to read the word.

One day, my mom picked me up from school early. I thought maybe we were going to the dentist, which I love because I get to wear sunglasses and watch TV while lying down. But we didn't go to the dentist. We went to a building I had never been to before.

I met a lady named Dr. Laura. We played together and read books. We talked about words and sounds. It wasn't scary. She was really nice. Still, it made me kind of nervous when Dr. Laura wrote in her notebook. When we were done, I got to play in a room with lots of toys while my mom and Dr. Laura talked.

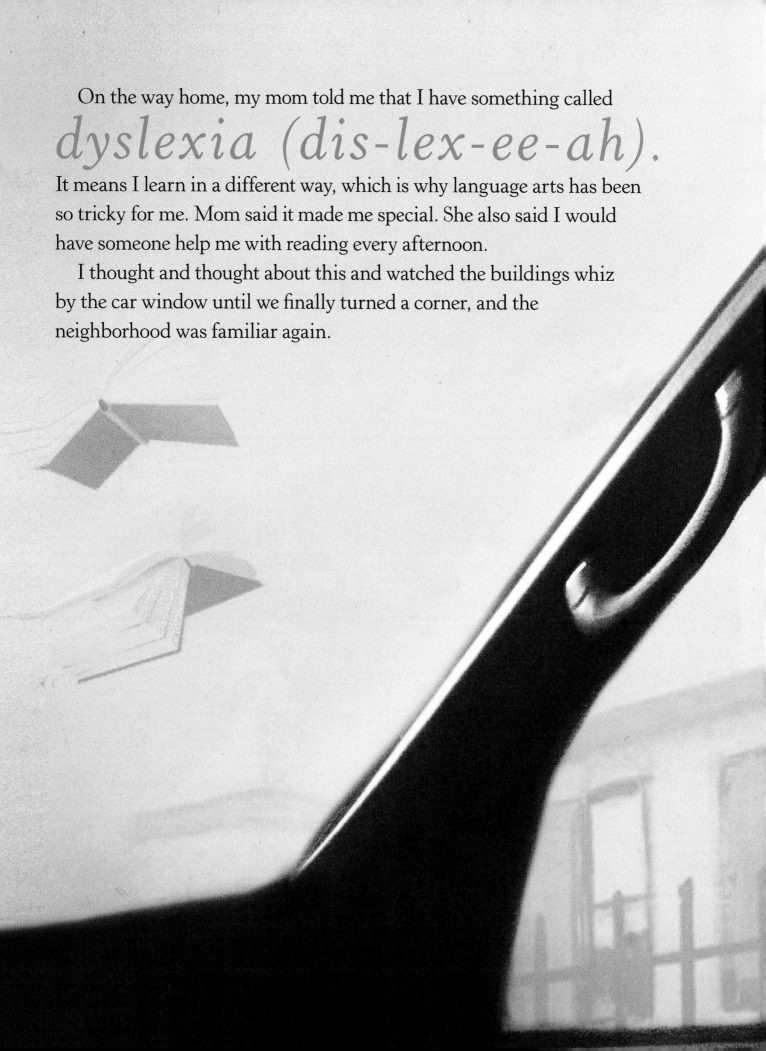

On the way home, my mom told me that I have something called *dyslexia (dis-lex-ee-ah)*. It means I learn in a different way, which is why language arts has been so tricky for me. Mom said it made me special. She also said I would have someone help me with reading every afternoon.

I thought and thought about this and watched the buildings whiz by the car window until we finally turned a corner, and the neighborhood was familiar again.

Mom made my favorite dinner that night—spaghetti with meatballs, which always makes me happy. But I still felt confused about this new thing. Dyslexia. It didn't sound like something anybody was lucky to have.

And I wasn't feeling very special.

My brother Josh is special because he has a superpower.

His superpower is kindness. He uses it to make other people smile and feel happy inside. Dyslexia wasn't making me feel powerful, and I was pretty sure I couldn't use it to make other people feel happy inside.

I decided to ask my mom for more information. She knows a lot about things. "Mommy, do I have to get extra help because I'm stupid?"

"No, of course not!" she said. "Having dyslexia doesn't mean you're stupid. It means you learn differently, and you see the world differently. And that might just be your special superpower."

"In fact, Abigail, you're exceptionally intelligent."

Intelligent means really smart.

"How can dyslexia be a superpower?"

"When everyone else is looking at a problem or a situation one way, you'll be looking at it from an entirely different angle. That means you'll be able to see solutions other people don't. You'll be able to spot hidden potential and hidden paths."

Potential is all the great things that you could be and you could do.

I liked the sound of this.

But I felt doubtful. I wanted to believe her, though...
isn't that what moms are supposed to say?

She must have been able to see all the questions on my face because she grabbed a book out of her bag and opened it. She told me Dr. Laura gave her this book about dyslexia so she can understand how I learn. Mom pointed to a page in the book where she had written the words in red pen that said, "Abigail to a T."

"What does that mean?" I asked.

"It means this describes you perfectly," she said. "And it doesn't say anything in here about kids with dyslexia being stupid."

My mom read the page to me and explained some things she learned about people who have dyslexia. I found out that my superpower makes me...

Superpowers of People Who Are Dyslexic

1.
Think with pictures instead of words.

2.
Instead of only seeing things how they are, my brain can see the way things could be.

3.
Very aware of the things around me.

4.
Able to understand things by listening to my heart.

5.
Understand things better by
using all of my senses.

6.
Super-duper imaginative.

7.
Extremely curious about
the world.

Abigail to a T

This is
why I ask lots
of questions!

My superpower was starting to sound really great.

"In fact," said my mom, "did you know that many famous inventors, artists, and engineers had dyslexia?"

"Really?!" I couldn't believe it!

"It's true." She pointed to another page in the book. "People like Albert Einstein, who developed the theory of relativity,

Steven Spielberg,
who makes brilliant films

Ann Bancroft, who was the first woman to cross the Arctic ice and reach the North Pole on dogsled

Pablo Picasso, who created some of
the most fascinating works of art and
Alexander Graham Bell, who invented
the telephone.''

"So they did cool things even though they had dyslexia?" I asked.

"No, Abigail. They achieved great things because of their dyslexia," said Mom. "It was this gift that allowed them to create and think in new and creative ways. This was their superpower. And it's your superpower, too."

WHOA.

This made me think about dyslexia differently.

But I still had more questions.

"Mom, then why do I need extra help to learn to read?"

"Well," she said, "superheroes need different tools than everyone else.
Your tutor will help you use your dyslexia. It's not something you
need to overcome. It's a gift! You just need to learn how to use it."

"Am I going to grow out of it?"

"No, Abigail. You'll never grow out of it. It will be your superpower forever. We're going to help you grow into it."

I grew into my sister's old roller skates. I grew into broccoli. (I used to hate it!) And I'm finally tall enough to ride big-kid roller coasters. But I've never grown into a superpower before.

Mom hugged me. Soon after that, Josh popped his head into my room. "Want to see my new dance move?" he asked.
"Of course!" I said. (The answer is always, of course!)

Josh played his new favorite song on his cell phone and danced around in circles. He became so shiny that I could feel myself beginning to shine also.

Then he sat next to me on my bed. "Hey, I heard you have a superpower too."
I nodded my head. Talking to Josh felt like a warm hug.

"That's really great," he said.

"Why is it great?" I asked.

"Because superheroes work better in pairs.
It's about time I had a sidekick."

This made me smile so big.
I always wanted to be more like Josh. I think we make a pretty good team.
    Having dyslexia doesn't feel so lonely anymore. When I think about it as
a way to look at the world in a new way, solve problems, and help others, it
makes me feel SUPER POWERful.

Monica Berg

Mother, wife, sister, daughter, teacher, friend, author, podcaster, cardio enthusiast and Change Junkie, Monica integrates all that she is into her mission of sharing with others. Monica is a fresh voice that channels the powerful internal spark of Light living within us all.

Authentic and fearless, she reminds us of our extraordinary potential and pushes us onward with compassion and understanding.

While informed by her many years of kabbalistic study, Monica also draws heavily on her own personal life experiences. She battled and overcame a debilitating eating disorder at a young age, and as a mother of four children, one of whom has special needs, she has become an outspoken advocate for him and others struggling to find their voice.

Grant Friedman

With her trademark blend of humor, insight, and honesty, she shows individuals how to create a life that feels like it is working, like it makes sense, and most importantly, a life in which they are living and loving as the powerful, fulfilled person they've always wanted to be. Her personal endeavors have taught her how the practical wisdom of Kabbalah can bring Light and strength into even the most challenging experiences by changing the one thing we can control, ourselves.

Monica Berg, a self-professed Change Junkie, shares her combination of wisdom and real-life awareness with talks found compelling to a wide range of people at different stages in their lives. She leads people to not only see how they can change (change is the only constant in life) but inspires them to get excited about a lifestyle of change.

Monica Berg is the author of *Fear Is Not an Option* and *Rethink Love,* co-hosts the Spiritually Hungry podcast, and serves as Co-director and Chief Communications Officer for Kabbalah Centre International. She lives in New York with her husband Michael and their children David, Joshua, Miriam, and Abigail.

Abigail Berg

At 8 years old, Abigail Berg is making her writing debut as the co-creator of *The Gift of Being Different*. The book was conceived before she could even read or write. When Abigail was diagnosed with dyslexia, she chose not to let dyslexia define her. Instead, she would redefine what it means to be different. Since then, Abigail has strived to be a role model for those who feel like they don't quite fit in, which, she has discovered, is most people. Abigail's hope is for all people, young and old, to embrace their differences and transform them into their own personal superpowers. The youngest of four siblings, Abigail lives in NYC with her parents, siblings, and her dog Miles.

Ivy Reynolds

Andrea Zarrella

Sonia Possentini

Italian illustrator and painter Sonia Maria Luce Possentini graduated with a degree in Art History from the Academy of Fine Arts in Bologna. During her studies, Sonia received scholarships from the prestigious Magnani Rocca Foundation and Olands Grafiska Skola of Venice. She further refined her artistry under master illustrator Štěpán Zavřel Kveta Pacovska. Sonia has illustrated over 200 children's books, and her work has been featured in publications around the world. She has received numerous awards, including the MAM Masters of Art and Craft Award, Andersen Prize for best illustrator, the Cento-Ferrara International Illustration award, and first prize by the International Children's Illustration Competition.

Sonia currently resides in Prignano sulla Secchia in the Modena Province of Italy with her partner and their two dogs, Mia and Nina. When not illustrating or painting, she can be found roaming the hills and meadows of the Modena Apennines and tending her garden. Sonia is represented by MB Artist in the U.S.

Dedication

I dedicate this book to all the children and former children in the world who, at one point or another, felt judged, weird, excluded, different, ostracized, or stupid. My wish is that we all come to love and accept our differences so completely that we see them as the gifts that they are.

And to my dearest children David, Joshua, Miriam, and Abigail, you have and continue to inspire me every day of your lives from the moment you entered mine. Through aiding you in navigating this world and helping you realize your powerful, individual, and unique potentials, you have helped me more fully realize my own.

Thank you, Michael, for being the best life partner that one could have and for bringing these special souls into the world with me.

A special thanks to Jazmine Aluma, who helped me articulate my message, Jason Sechrest for his keen ear and sharp editing, Josh Beatman, whose experience and advice have helped me navigate this undertaking, Liz Tippit for being my wing woman in helping me manifest all things near and dear to my heart and to the extraordinarily talented Sonia Maria Luce Possentini, whose illustrations brought the story to life.

And extra special thanks to Abigail, my co-creator, muse, daughter, and partner, whose journey inspired this book. Abigail, you inspire me every day with your thoughtful spirit, kindness, strength, and brilliance.

ISBN 979-8-9859200-0-0 (Hardcover Edition)
Art by Sonia Possentini • Design by Josh Beatman/Brainchild Studios
First printing July 2022 • Printed in the United States of America
Published by Spiritually Hungry Publishing
Spiritually Hungry Publishing is a dba of Kabbalah Centre International, Inc.
info@spirituallyhungrypublishing.com